hedgerow #144
a journal of small poems

edited by Caroline Skanne

Copyright © 2023 Caroline Skanne

All rights revert to respective authors & artists upon publication. No work featured here may be used, copied, sold or distributed elsewhere without permission.

ISBN: 9798871118634

published by:
wildflower poetry press

www.wildflowerpoetrypress.com

hedgerowhaiku.com

cover photograph 'screes' & design: Caroline Skanne
editor: Caroline Skanne

hedgerow is a short-poetry journal dedicated to publishing an eclectic mix of new and established voices across the spectrum of the short poem, with particular attention to English-language haiku & related works.

As always, while submissions are read on a rolling basis, submission reminders are emailed out ahead of each issue. If you are not currently on the mailing list, simply send an email with the subject heading 'subscribe' to:

hedgerowsubmission@gmail.com

far from home
still some warmth
in the stone

pouring rain
the palm-sized kitten
begins to purr

Evan Vandermeer

autumn evening—
my sternum still marked
by the cello's rim

Philip Rowland

each breath
breaking the silence
mountains under new snow

autumn moving into winter
all the picture hooks removed
from the wall

Gary Hotham

church bells . . .
the rooftop pigeons
continue their preening

prairie wind—
hay bales weigh down
a field of alfalfa

Julie Schwerin

peeling figs
the cat's tail slightly
waves to my song

Keiko Izawa

the pebble's descent
from the cliff to the lake
I finally quit

Meagan Bussert

a tinge of light
the sunflower field
at dusk

Pat Davis

city library
a book of death poems
in the new arrivals

Alvin B. Cruz

still looking around
for the one who is not here . . .
off leash park

Madhuri Pillai

roadside . . .
the fading light
of a badger

Rob Kingston

staring at mother
staring out the window
retirement home

Juan Edgardo De Pascuale

street musician
playing the B-sides
of memory

Judson Evans

a breeze carries
the fresh smell of apples
last summer swim

Aaron Bowker

blackberry lemonade
the bruises
took weeks to heal

Joshua St. Claire

adding old socks
to the dishrag pile
spring rain

Carly Siegel Thorp

thunderstorm
bunched-up sheets
at the bottom of the bed

a trail
through horsetail
whispering creek

Brad Bennett

        where the road curves
             the softest part
                 of a folk tune

uptick in red knots
the wind lifts
a closed beach notice

Anne Burgevin

autumn night
filling an unlit room
the cat's purr

Gordon Brown

desire
is not enough
birdsong

not trying
not to look
skinny dipping

Jeff Hoagland

bushtits in the birches
a morning of back and forth
emails

suburban stars
the late fee
waived

Tanya McDonald

dust motes
the stillness
of the pendulum clock

Frank Hooven

april mist
resilience
in silence

new snow
old snow
shadow play

David Kāwika Eyre

oolong unfurling
just one more thing defined
by what it's not

Bob Lucky

minute's silence—
passing geese
too far to be heard

in the graveyard
writing
a 'to do' list

John Gonzalez

in the wing whistle
of a mourning dove
waning summer

Helen Ogden

oranges falling
in the square
kids play football

Claire Thom

scented breeze from another village church bells

Stephen Toft

wood stove
the cat
claims the closest seat

Lee Hudspeth

evening clouds
wishing for stars
to wish on

Ben Gaa

after the fighter jets
a flock
of geese

our train through vanishing vastness

Tom Clausen

drought
a tiny pond
holding the sky

summer rain
on the clothesline
her sun hat

Karen Robbie

after sunset . . .
a song once sung
from the backseat

Jamie Wimberly

chatting all the way migrating geese

the pine where do i begin

th. vandergrau

autumn beach
an abandoned shell necklace
on the shore

Eufemia Griffo

empty nester—
and from now on
only take-aways

Katja Fox

astronauts
go about their work
snow in the pines

a horse standing
perfectly still
could be sun could be moon

Peter Yovu

Chidambar Navalgund (poem) & *Shloka Shankar* (art)

Ding-a-Ling

Not a job I'd like. Helping people write their wills. Still, seen it all by now, I reckon. "So, one last thing," she says. "Let's talk about donating."

    estate sale
    each murky jar
    labelled in Latin

Some leave their brains. Others, whatever organ is likely to cause death—lungs are popular. Hearts, too. Or, and she smiles, I can go for the whole shebang. Donate my body. I'm thinking lock stock and bollocks.

    butcher's block . . .
    scooping offal trimmings
    into Nan's wetbag

Her family grins from a photo behind her desk. Some may now be dead, lying on slabs or packed into freezers. I hear myself cough. "Not for me," I whisper. Then louder, "Nowt. Nada."

"Are you sure? I mean, your wife has …"

    at the end of the postnup nothing left

"But what if I'm not dead?" I say. "Might only be sleeping or something. Then someone comes along and saws my head off. Or slices me open and … I mean, why d'you think I chose cremation? Too late then, ain't it? A quick bit of searing pain, and 'bye! Better than being lowered alive next to Mam and Dad."

    blue sky
    a scent of ponderosa
    from the pyre

She smiles, folds her arms. "Have you considered a coffin bell?"

Lew Watts

Slipping Glimpsers

They say human consciousness took a great leap forward when, some 700 years ago, Petrarch chose to climb Mont Ventoux for nothing other than the view. Like him, I too have had what might be called an elevated experience at an unusual height, but mine was atop a grassy hill next to a McDonald's, where my dad would take me for lunch after my little league baseball games. One afternoon, as the two of us sat and talked with our meals nearly finished, the normally constant traffic streaming below us stopped, and for a few breathless seconds—fries suspended halfway to our gaping mouths—the whole world paused, it seemed, and emptied of sound, as if by some marvelous blip in the system. Neither of us shared what happened with the rest of the family, and if we had, it would probably have sounded just as unremarkable as it does now.

    morning dark
    a distant train's whistle
    through the zendo

    Evan Vandermeer

carved
into my headstone
a map to the saint's house
to the stars
from beverly hills, only $5

leafshiver
in the halting of moments
a distant hush
wild waves wist
above the solstice nest

sugar craving
my flesh through the holes
of the fishnets
I wrap the cakes differently depending
on who's receiving the cake

Jennifer Hambrick
& *Richard Gilbert*

A Moon Ago

aged out
in the bud
autumn roses

*a walking rope of toddlers
through falling leaves*

jet thunder
my under-desk memories
resurface

*pulled over
for a funeral procession
I check my watch*

in darkened skies
rainbow hunting

*a moon ago
how far this sunflower
would turn*

John Thompson
& *Chuck Brickley*

Mimi Kunz

I turn
to wait for you
on the path
the forget-me-nots
flowering

Colin Oliver

                                                woodland diary
                                                all bark and light
                                                leaves and song
                                                the brush of river
                                                or is it sky

                                                Joanna Ashwell

autumn wind
weaves through a forest
in a dream . . .
the creek still carries
her whispers

her story
within a story
this autumn night . . .
layers of fog
hiding the mountain

Jacob D. Salzer

my x-rayed skull—
in noon sun
men drop scaffolding
down the side of
a newly painted building

Philip Rowland

that place
in the diagnosis
between knowing
and not knowing . . .
a dimly lit corridor

Cherie Hunter Day

to belong again
to this house
and its laughter —
the curtains of my room
are autumn's burnt umber

Alan Peat

gone to seed
these past memories
I still dream
of my father gathering
the last of his crops

Pris Campbell

on our drive
through the autumn hills
my silent note of the photos
I'd stop to take
if I was alone

Tom Clausen

deep breathing
my way to wellness
offshore
whales exhale towards
an uncertain future

Carole MacRury

taking down
the paper lanterns
the cold whisper
of autumn
chills

the sunset
now belongs
to me
and
this house

ai li

BODY
after The Necks (24.46 minutes in)

as though a door burst open
in a room you hadn't known
you were in

Philip Rowland

                                                                           wall of room
                                                                           wall of space

                                                                           walled in
                                                                           walled up

                                                                           walled out
                                                                           of touch

                                                                           I feel
                                                                           a way

                                                                           .

                                                                           eye drops
                                                                           beside

                                                                           the ink
                                                                           bottle

                                                                           John Martone

in spite

        an inventory

of everything

        of archetypes

nil desperandum

        in the storehouse
        of nothing

.

the female body—
fill-in-the-adjective-of-your-choice

Shloka Shankar

                                          a cat
                                          on
                                          the roof

                                          sniffing
                                          the air

                                          of plum wine

                                          ai li

the high I'm always chasing summer clouds

Bryan Rickert

ant column . . .
a dung beetle
pauses its roll

Adjei Agyei-Baah

dry sargassum
the shell left behind
by a moulting crab

Bill Cooper

winter light
wallaby bones whiter
in a patch of sun

Lorraine Haig

eyes open all night long praying mantis

Randy Brooks

psalms
from the greige of fog
wild geese

Beverly Acuff Momoi

sunflower heads dropping a note about dad

Alan Peat

nightingale's warble
her sobs
a little quieter

Kelly Sargent

his bible
gold leaf on the pages
worn thin

Robert Moyer

late session
the drip of an icicle
outside the window

Roland Packer

a faint woody scent
from the stationery shop
autumn evening

Daniela Misso

angel for sale
wings
slightly bent

Christine Eales

her prayer book
the *Memorare* marked
with an Edelweiss

Sarah Paris

pre-dawn drive
turkeys following deer
up the dark ravine

Dyana Basist

a mystery novel
left open on the table
migrating geese

promises to keep
a trailside flicker feather
points south

a silent key
on the old piano
evening fog

Kristen Lindquist

candlelit vigil
the gun
wedged at his waist

unmade bed . . .
the wingbeats
of a swan

Aidan Castle

autumn chill
the butter resists
the knife

morning sunlight
the crows feast
on windfall apples

Erica Ison

late harvest . . .
a kestrel watches
from the wires

Clive Bennett

lost among
the mustard fields . . .
goldfinch

zen garden . . .
raking over
the rabbit's tracks

Carole MacRury

spring sun
a grain of grit
in my shoe

David Gale

frogs singing
between car noise
the smell of lilac

Christer Hansson

thrift store
the old globe
smells of smoke

Nathanael Tico

ruffled feathers
in the osprey nest
summer storm

Meg Arnot

counterglow

   there
     is
   no

   other

the way Cliff Scott's sax lays
back on the beat
nows

rust
in the gate's creak
a late cricket

Chuck Brickley

blues guitar
at the beach shack
a pod of dolphins
cruises the bay

Vanessa Proctor

the partial eclipse
   hidden by clouds, I serve up
      sun-dried tomatoes

John Martone

late morning
a friend tells me about
the supermoon

Frank Williams

creeping juniper
the slip
of tectonic plates

Eric Sundquist

flowers fade
and yet . . .
one cricket

Carole Johnston

crescent moonlight—
intending to be lucid
in my dreams tonight

mountain wildflower slope—
how my life could be
one long poem

Rebecca Lilly

I shake the sand
out of my walking shoes—
early autumn rain

Maeve O'Sullivan

not lost
but not found either
waning crescent moon

Alanna C. Burke

unilateral disarmament
roses replaced
by milkweed

Sharon R. Wesoky

wind gusts
a piglet nestles
in the girl's arms

Claire Vogel Camargo

summer night
a slug eats through
the tomato seedling

Gordon Gearhart

family reunion
inquiring about people
not here

Barbara Tate Sayre

                end of summer
                a few grains of sand
                in the empty drawers

                Daniel Birnbaum

day beginning—
the delicate legs
of a cellar spider

Goran Gatalica

        from a paper cup his ashes in a winding river

        Deborah Bowman

long way home
a halo of sun
through snow mist

Jay Friedenberg

local hardware store
the sanctity of buying
just what you need

j rap

waves of mist . . .
abandoned
mud swallow nests

Jennifer Burd

graveside
stumbling to the end
of the poem

Benedict Grant

deep winter
the painter's palette
black and white

Stephanie Zepherelli

latchkey the lives we planned

geese overhead
the lock keeper
pauses

pub bin
a crow pulling a crisp packet
through the snow

frances angela

                                        father's gravestone
                                        nobody else to remember
                                        him bowling

                                        in the vastness of the universe
                                        there's a troubling spot
                                        on his white shirt

                                        Howard Colyer

into the jagged edges of my psyche night jasmine

Surashree Joshi

picking up
where we left off
winter breeze

Laurie D. Morrissey

cemetery visit . . .
now a year older
than mum

mid-winter
yesterday's dishes
in the sink

Jo McInerney

dawn stars . . .
clatters of coins fill
the snack stand

old temple
the Buddha polished
by visitors' hands

David He Zhuanglang

somewhere
above the thinning . . .
a bluebird's sunlit call

Kathryn Liebowitz

wasting time
where the river bends
honeysuckle

Mark Forrester

sunshower
finding a rainbow
that's almost not there

Ruth Holzer

autumn mountain
somehow all the colours
with a hint of blue

Iliyana Stoyanova

first fall night
last green tomato
plucked from the vine

Deborah A. Bennett

marking white lines
on the grass
distant mountains

Seth

weekend retreat
just enough rice
for one

petrichor
which book
next

Matthew Caretti

these last
autumn days
making small talk

Lee Felty

hard rain
the grey of it
indoors

Tony Williams

autumn leaves—
the thrill of the first bike ride
without training wheels

spots of bare earth
in a field of snow
the palomino's frosty breath

Joseph P. Wechselberger

high tide's quiet . . .
drizzle adds its weight
to a harebell's droop

dense woodland finding the way as i am

soft peat deep pools time taking time

Thomas Powell

oppressive heat
the mid-day church bells
disperse dust

Maya Daneva

someone else your selfie

morning after
    a stack of moving boxes
            leans on another

Victor Ortiz

                          crane migration
                          an unexplained urge
                          to hop in the car

                          Mike Stinson

how the mind works
sound of the foghorn
long gone

Jill Lange

                    dawn stirring the roosting tree's wings

                    heat after the rain
                    swans come ashore
                    to preen

                    Polona Oblak

grief an ancient dialect of snow

the uneven drawstring cinching winter

Cherie Hunter Day

grass
on a mother's grave
wind from the mountain

scent of oil
the cool darkness
of a country garage

Liam Carson

nothing left to say—
dark swirls of kelp
on a shifting tide

shift in the wind—
thousands of jellyfish
vanish overnight

Amanda Bell

Printed in Great Britain
by Amazon